FOR THOSE
WHO
KNOW

RAJAN DOMINARI

FOR THOSE WHO KNOW

A BOOK OF DOMINANCE, DISCIPLINE, AND DEVOTION

NOT FOR THE CURIOUS.
ONLY FOR THE CALLED.

RAVEN ROW PRESS

R.

Published by Raven Row Press

This is a work of non-fiction, written to offer encouragement, mentorship, and practical guidance to those navigating Dominant/submissive relationships. The views expressed reflect the author's personal insights and lived experience, and are intended for informational and inspirational purposes only. This book is not a substitute for professional, medical, psychological, or legal advice.

First Edition: 2025
ISBN (Paperback): 978-1-7345271-5-5

Cover art and book design by Studio Pedroza
Interior layout and formatting by Studio Pedroza

Printed and published in the United States of America.

For Dominant Desires-specific inquiries, contact:
domdesiresofficial@gmail.com

For permissions, inquiries, or bulk orders, please contact:
Raven Row Press
ravenrow@akopublishing.com

For the ones who carry the weight,

and the ones who choose to yield.

INTRODUCTION

This book isn't here to flatter you.

It isn't made to validate the soft fantasies of roleplayers or stroke the egos of men who mistake control for command.

These pages are for the few—for the Dominants who lead with integrity, the submissives who offer their obedience with meaning, and the couples who live by standards that most will never understand.

What follows is not a manual. It is a measure.

Each entry cuts through the noise. A quote. A reflection. A truth.

If you feel exposed, good. If something stings, better. If you find yourself nodding in silence, welcome. You belong here.

This world isn't for everyone.
And that's exactly the point.

There is no freedom in submission without trust,
no honour in Dominance without restraint.

Rajan Dominari

I.

HE DOESN'T PLAY WITH POWER.
HE CARRIES IT.

There's a difference between wearing the look and owning the weight. Between posing like a Dominant and moving like one. The real ones don't need props. Their presence is the pressure. Their gaze is the leash.

She knew it the moment he looked at her—not with hunger, but with intent. He wasn't reacting to her. He was deciding. And when a man like that makes a decision, the whole room feels it.

2.

OBEDIENCE IS NOT SUBMISSION.
ONE CAN BE TRAINED. THE OTHER
MUST BE EARNED.

Obedience is an action. Submission is a gift. The difference is in the soul of it. Anyone can be taught to follow orders, to kneel, to mimic the motions. But submission—that's something deeper. It doesn't come from conditioning. It comes from trust.

True Dominants know that distinction. They don't crave performance. They crave surrender that is freely given, not taken through fear or force. The moment she chooses to yield—not because she must, but because she wants to—is the moment it becomes real.

3.

I AM NOT HER EQUAL. I AM HER EDGE.

Equality is a fine word for polite society. But in the quiet confines of this world, something different unfolds. She doesn't want balance. She wants contrast. She wants someone who doesn't mirror her—but challenges her, contains her, completes her by countering her.

To be her edge is to be the boundary she leans into, the force she tests herself against. Not to overpower her, but to draw something out of her that only exists in the presence of strength. You are the edge—sharp enough to define her, firm enough to hold her.

4.

PAIN IS NOT PUNISHMENT. PAIN IS POETRY.

To the untrained eye, the strike looks cruel. But those who live within this world understand: it is expression. It is rhythm. It is sacred and chosen. Pain, when laced with care and control, becomes language. A way of saying I see you. I shape you.

There is nothing chaotic in the whip that lands with purpose. Nothing brutal in the slap that leaves her breathless and blooming. When pain is crafted, it becomes art. Not to break her spirit—but to awaken it.

5.

SHE DOESN'T KNEEL BECAUSE
SHE'S SMALL. SHE KNEELS BECAUSE
SHE'S STRONG ENOUGH TO LOWER
HERSELF.

Weakness has no place in submission. The ones who kneel do so from strength—because they could stand, but choose not to. It's a paradox the world struggles to understand: that surrender can be the most powerful thing a woman does.

Kneeling is not an act of defeat. It's a moment of clarity. She knows who she is. She knows who he is. And in that knowing, she bends. Not from pressure, but from purpose.

6.

HER BODY IS MINE—BECAUSE
SHE GAVE IT TO ME. AND I AM
RESPONSIBLE FOR EVERYTHING I DO
WITH IT.

Ownership in this life isn't metaphor. It's the mark of a woman who has handed over the reins—not because she's weak, but because she knows who deserves them. When she yields, she's not losing herself. She's choosing to be claimed by a man worthy of that role.

But ownership doesn't excuse indulgence. A real Dominant doesn't hide behind power—he holds it with discipline. Her body is yours, yes—but only as long as you treat it like it matters. Because it does.

7.

I'LL TAKE HER APART, BUT I'LL PUT HER BACK TOGETHER BETTER.

There is a dismantling that isn't destruction. There's a tearing down that doesn't break—it clears the way. He doesn't ruin her. He removes the pieces she no longer needs. The defences. The doubt. The distractions.

When she emerges, she's still hers—but she's also his. Sharper. Softer. More whole in her surrender than she ever was in her armour. This is the paradox of being undone: that in losing herself, she finds more.

8.

SHE CALLS ME 'SIR' BECAUSE I'VE EARNED IT, NOT BECAUSE I EXPECT IT.

Titles without meaning mean nothing. Anyone can demand them. Not everyone is worth them. Sir is not a performance—it's a recognition. She offers it when she feels held, challenged, respected, and claimed.

There's nothing forced about real respect. It rises from how he leads, how he listens, how he carries the weight of her trust without cracking. When she calls him Sir, she's naming not his role, but his worth.

9.

PUNISHMENT WITHOUT PURPOSE IS
CRUELTY. PURPOSE WITHOUT PAIN
IS WASTED.

There's a difference between using pain as a tool and wielding it as a weapon. The point is not to make her suffer—it's to teach, to centre, to correct, to remind. Discipline is a language between two people who understand the deeper rules beneath the surface.

But for it to mean something, it has to hurt. Not arbitrarily. Not carelessly. But sharply enough that the lesson stays. A punishment without pain is just a lecture. And no one kneels for a lecture.

10.

HER SUBMISSION IS NOT MINE TO TAKE. IT'S MINE TO DESERVE.

This is the foundation everything else is built upon. You can tie her wrists. You can command her breath. But if you haven't earned her yes, you've earned nothing. She is not yours until she chooses to be.

And when she does—fully, freely—her submission becomes sacred. It is the ultimate offering: not demanded, not coerced, but willingly placed at your feet. To lead her after that is not a privilege. It's a vow.

II.

SHE DOESN'T WANT TO BE RESCUED.
SHE WANTS TO BE RUINED—
PROPERLY.

There is a kind of ruin that isn't damage—it's devotion. She doesn't long for a man who saves her from herself. She longs for one who sees all of her, unearths the layers she hides, and claims what's beneath without flinching.

This isn't about being broken. It's about being remade through surrender. To be ruined by someone who knows what they're doing, who touches her with intent, who pushes with purpose—that is where she feels most alive.

12.

A DOMINANT EARNS HER SUBMISSION—AND CONTINUES EARNING THE RIGHT TO KEEP IT.

She may offer it freely, but she's watching. Submission isn't a gift wrapped in naivety—it's a mirror of how you lead. The title means nothing without the follow-through.

Any man can call himself a Dominant. Only a few can carry it without cracking. Because the moment he forgets what her trust costs her to give, he stops deserving it.

13.

SHE DOESN'T KNEEL BECAUSE SHE'S TOLD TO. SHE KNEELS BECAUSE SHE NEEDS TO.

It isn't just obedience. It's oxygen. In a world that demands she lead, climb, and conquer—kneeling is her exhale. Her return to centre. Her choice to hand over the weight for a while and let herself be instead of do.

He never needs to remind her. Her body remembers. Her bones remember. And when the rest of the world is too loud, the floor beneath her and his voice above her are the only things that make sense.

14.

HIS STRENGTH ISN'T IN HIS
DOMINANCE. IT'S IN HOW HE
CARRIES HER SUBMISSION.

Anyone can give orders. However, not everyone can be trusted with surrender. What makes him strong is not his ability to command—but how seriously he takes the weight of being obeyed. He doesn't see her submission as a prize. He sees it as a vow.

There is grace in his firmness. Restraint in his fire. And when he tells her what to do, it's never from ego. It's from responsibility. She follows not because she fears him—but because she trusts he won't misuse the power she's placed in his hands.

15.

THEY AREN'T EQUALS IN POWER.
THEY ARE EQUALS IN PURPOSE.

The dynamic is not symmetrical—but it is balanced. One leads, one yields. But both are aligned in what they seek: intimacy, discipline, devotion, truth. Power isn't split evenly—it's directed intentionally.

She thrives in her submission. He steadies in his command. And together, they move in a rhythm that makes sense only to them. That is equality of a different kind—not based on sameness, but on significance.

16.

HE GIVES HER RULES SO SHE CAN
FINALLY REST.

She doesn't want chaos. She wants clarity. And when he gives her structure, she exhales. No guessing. No overthinking. No pretending to lead when all she wants is to follow something steady.

Rules aren't cages. They're comfort. They mean someone is paying attention. They mean she matters enough to correct. And when she obeys, it's not fear—it's relief.

17.

HE DOESN'T NEED TO RAISE HIS
VOICE. SHE ALREADY HEARS HIM
EVERYWHERE.

She can feel him in the silence. The way her hands fall to her lap. The way she hesitates before making a choice. The echo of his discipline lingers—not just in memory, but in muscle.

This is not about domination through volume. It's presence. Precision. Influence so refined it becomes reflex. He doesn't have to demand her obedience anymore. He's already become the gravity she moves within.

18.

HER DEFIANCE IS NOT A THREAT.
IT'S A BRIEF TEST OF DEPTH—NOT A
PERMISSION TO PUSH LIMITS.

True submission is not silence, but it is respect and discipline. Early on, she may challenge—seeking to understand the boundaries, to feel the strength behind the command. This is not rebellion; it is cautious vetting.

A true Dominant does not indulge defiance or let it become habit. He meets it with unwavering calm and clear boundaries, proving that strength is steadiness, not anger. This is how trust is built—and how limits are honoured.

19.

THEY UNDRESS WITH PURPOSE, NOT URGENCY.

This is not about speed. This is not about need. This is about attention. Every button, every breath, every pause says something. The removal of clothing is a ceremony. A stripping down of ego and armour.

There's a difference between being naked and being seen. They aim for the latter. Because in this world, the body is not only a thing to use. It's a language to speak.

20.

SHE'S NOT WEAK BECAUSE SHE
YIELDS. SHE'S POWERFUL BECAUSE
SHE CHOOSES TO.

There's nothing small about her. Nothing passive. Submission is not her default—it's her decision. And that decision carries weight. She can walk away. She can say no. The fact that she doesn't is what makes her dangerous.

Power isn't always loud. Sometimes it kneels. Sometimes it waits. And sometimes, it looks you in the eye and says, I trust you. Don't make me regret it.

21.

HE DOESN'T TAKE CONTROL. HE BECOMES IT.

Real dominance doesn't announce itself. It arrives. Quiet. Certain. The kind of presence that doesn't need to prove anything because it's already been felt.

She doesn't follow him because he tells her to. She follows because something in her recognises him. Something deep. Animal. Ancient. It isn't performance. It's possession—worn like a second skin.

22.

HER BODY REMEMBERS WHAT HER
PRIDE TRIES TO FORGET.

She'll talk back. She'll argue. She'll test the edges. But the moment his hand touches her neck, or his voice drops into that command—her mind stills. Her muscles soften. Her breathing changes.

It isn't about control. It's about connection that bypasses logic. Something older than language. She can posture all she wants—her body has already chosen him.

23.

THERE IS NO SHAME IN OBEDIENCE WHEN IT'S EARNED.

Obedience isn't submission without thought. It's the end of doubt. The moment she chooses yes, not from fear, but from faith. Because he's proven himself. Because he's consistent. Because he's built the kind of safety that sharpens her, not softens her.

There's pride in how she listens. In how she moves. Obedience isn't weakness—it's trust in motion.

24.

THEY DON'T FALL INTO BED. THEY FALL INTO PLACE.

Sex isn't an accident for them. It's a ritual. A realignment. The way he holds her down is the way he anchors her in the rest of their life. The way she gives herself isn't about pleasure—it's about belonging.

Every act is layered. Every sound is a story. It's not just heat— it's history. It's who they are when the rest of the world is peeled away.

25.

HE USES SILENCE THE WAY OTHERS
USE ROPE.

He doesn't need to bind her wrists. He binds her with his stillness. The way he looks at her without blinking. The way he waits for her to break the silence—just to feel her own need echoing back.

Power doesn't always speak. Sometimes it watches. Sometimes it lets the weight of the moment press down until she begs for the next word. Or the next strike. Or the next instruction.

26.

SHE ACHES NOT TO BE TAKEN—BUT
TO BE UNDERSTOOD AS SOMETHING
WORTH TAKING.

She's not a prize. She's a reckoning. And what she wants isn't blind lust—it's deliberate attention. She wants to be wanted in a way that sees her. Claimed in a way that feels earned. Not possessed by force, but chosen with precision.

She's not easy to hold. Not because she's difficult—but because she's deep. And if he can't meet her there, she'd rather go untouched than misunderstood.

27.

HE DISCIPLINES BECAUSE HE CARES.
HE'S CAREFUL BECAUSE HE OWNS.

To correct her is not cruelty—it's care. He doesn't punish to assert power. He punishes to protect the standard. To keep her anchored in what they've built. To keep her aligned with the woman she becomes through him.

And when it's over, he doesn't apologise. He doesn't retreat. He holds her tighter. Because ownership isn't about control. It's about responsibility. And that weight? He carries it without complaint.

28.

THEIR CONNECTION DOESN'T DIM IN PUBLIC. IT SIMMERS.

She walks beside him like any other woman might. But her glance, her silence, the way she shifts when he adjusts his tone—it's all there, just below the surface. D/s doesn't need chains to be present. It just needs two people who remember who they are, even when no one's watching.

He brushes her lower back. She straightens. He says her name a certain way. She lowers her eyes. This isn't performance. This is presence, under lock and key.

29.

SHE TESTS HIM WITH HER CHAOS.

HE ANSWERS WITH COMMAND.

She doesn't mean to unravel. It just happens. The days where her voice shakes, where her thoughts spiral, where nothing makes sense. That's when she needs him most. Not to soothe her—but to contain her.

He doesn't match her storm. He steadies it. One word. One rule. One unshakeable tone. And in that moment, she doesn't need comfort. She needs command. And he gives it without flinching.

30.

OBEDIENCE IS NOT THE ABSENCE OF
THOUGHT. IT'S THE PRESENCE OF
TRUST.

Anyone can follow out of fear. That's not obedience—that's survival. But when she yields to him, it's different. It's not about being told what to do. It's about believing that he knows—knows her, knows the moment, knows what matters.

31.

HE DOESN'T JUST WANT HER DEVOTION. HE WANTS HER DEPTH.

Devotion can be shallow. Performed. Learned. But he's not interested in obedience for its own sake. He wants to reach the part of her that resists—and win there. The place she hides, even from herself. He wants that part to kneel.

It's not about compliance. It's about truth. About who she is when the mask drops and the storm calms. That's where he lives. And that's what she gives, when it's real.

32.

HER OBEDIENCE IS NOT A RESPONSE
TO POWER. IT'S A REACTION TO
PRECISION.

She's not moved by volume. She's moved by accuracy. The way he notices. The way he adjusts. The way he speaks to her in a language no one else hears. Every command tailored. Every correction exact.

He doesn't dominate in general. He dominates her. With intention. With discipline. With detail. That's why she listens. That's why she yields. Because it's personal. And it's perfect.

33.

SOME NIGHTS, SHE NEEDS TO BE BROKEN. NOT FROM PAIN—BUT FROM PRESSURE.

It builds in her—the weight of being everything to everyone. The constant control. The sharp smile. The quiet fatigue. And then he appears, and she doesn't have to hold it anymore.

He doesn't ask. He just takes. Not her dignity—but her burden. He uses her body like a confession. Every moan, a release. Every bruise, a letting go. Until she's not empty—but free.

34.

DOMINANCE DOESN'T SEDUCE. IT REVEALS.

There's no performance here. No costume. Just presence. And clarity. The kind of energy that strips people down without laying a hand on them. It doesn't try to lure—it simply stands there, unapologetic, and watches who comes undone.

The right Dominant doesn't chase. He draws. Not because he's trying to convince—but because he already knows what he is. And so does she.

35.

SHE NEVER BEGGED TO BE OWNED.
BUT WHEN HE DID, IT FELT LIKE
HOME.

She didn't grow up dreaming of collars or kneeling at someone's feet. But when it happened—when the right man took her, held her, named her—it made sense in a way nothing else had.

Ownership, in his hands, was not reduction. It was recognition. A claiming that didn't confine, but clarified. She wasn't smaller beneath him. Just sharper. More whole. More hers. Through him.

36.

HE DIDN'T COMMAND HER.
HE MIMICKED COMMAND—ACTING
OUT A PERFORMANCE OF CONTROL.
AND SHE KNEW THE DIFFERENCE.

It's easy to play Dominant. Memorise some words. Copy a posture. Speak in a gravelly voice and call it control. But she knew better.

Real power doesn't posture—it penetrates.
It doesn't demand silence; it earns it.

He wasn't leading—he was pretending.
And she had no time for men who dress up in authority they haven't earned.

37.

SHE WORE SUBMISSION LIKE
LINGERIE—ONLY WHEN SOMEONE
WAS WATCHING.

There are women who kneel for attention. Who moan for the mirror. Who treat obedience like theatre. But submission isn't something you wear. It's something you carry. Quietly. Daily. Even when no one's looking.

The ones who live it don't have to prove it. It shows in their restraint. Their depth. Their loyalty when no praise is coming. And the men who know the difference? They don't chase the show. They choose the soul.

38.

HE TALKS ABOUT CONTROL BECAUSE HE'S NEVER HELD ANY.

Real Dominants don't need to explain power. They embody it. The louder he speaks of control, the more likely he's compensating for the lack. You can feel it—the overcorrection. The twitch behind the mask.

He doesn't correct her with calm. He lashes out with ego. He doesn't set structure. He sets traps. And when it all burns down, he'll say she was too much. But the truth? He was never enough.

39.

SOME CALL THEMSELVES SUBMISSIVE
JUST TO BE CENTRE STAGE IN
SOMEONE ELSE'S SHOW.

Not all kneeling is sincere. Some use it as currency. An aesthetic. A shortcut to power by way of feigned vulnerability. But service, when it's real, is rooted in something far deeper. It doesn't seek the spotlight. It protects the dynamic.

True submissives don't perform—they preserve. They bring strength to the structure, not chaos in lace. And the ones who truly serve? They don't need to tell you they're real. You just know.

40.

SHE DIDN'T NEED A THRONE.
SHE NEEDED A MAN WHO WOULDN'T
FALL FOR HER ACT.

She was used to getting her way. Used to being adored. But deep down, she craved something different—someone who saw through the sweetness, past the seduction. Someone who wouldn't be moved by her mask.

And when he didn't flinch... when he didn't fold or chase... when he stared right through her—she melted. Because that's the moment she finally felt seen. And finally felt safe.

41.

SHE DIDN'T WANT SAFETY.
SHE WANTED TO FEEL HELD—EVEN
WHEN IT HURT.

There's a difference between avoiding pain and being protected inside it. She didn't come to him to be spared discomfort. She came to be contained within it. To find someone who wouldn't flinch when she unraveled.

He didn't soothe her by softening the edges. He soothed her by staying. Staying when she cried. Staying when she begged. Staying when she trembled and gave him every jagged piece. And never once letting go.

42.

HE NEVER TOLD HER TO KNEEL.
HE MADE HER WANT TO.

Obedience is hollow when forced. He understood that. He didn't issue demands to hear himself talk. He moved with purpose, with weight, with the kind of presence that drew her to the floor without a word.

She wasn't submitting out of fear. She was responding to gravity. The kind only certain men carry—the kind that pulls the truth out of you, gently... and leaves you grateful to give it.

43.

SHE WAS SOFT IN THE PLACES HE
WAS HARD. AND THAT'S WHY THEY
FIT.

She didn't need to be remade. Just met. And he didn't need her to match his strength—he needed her to receive it. Her softness wasn't a flaw. It was the space his control could land and mean something.

She gave him her restraint. He gave her structure. And in that exchange, they didn't become opposites—they became whole. Not because they were the same. But because they remembered how to balance.

44.

HE SPOTTED HER COLLAR—BUT
WAITED TO SEE IF HER EYES
MATCHED IT.

Adornment is easy. Identity is not. Anyone can wear a collar. Few can live one. So he didn't move when he saw it. He watched. Waited. Measured the way she walked, listened, responded.

Because true submission can't be faked for long. Eventually, the act slips. The posture cracks. And when it does, he'll know. Not because she failed—but because he noticed. And that noticing? That's what separates him from the rest.

45.

WHEN SHE SURRENDERS,
SHE DOESN'T FALL. SHE LANDS.

Surrender, when it's real, isn't a loss. It's a return. A deliberate letting go into something stronger. Something trusted. Something earned. She doesn't collapse in his hands—she settles into them.

Because she knows who he is. She knows how far she can fall without being dropped. And that depth of surrender? It only comes from one thing: knowing that his hands were made to hold her.

46.

HE DIDN'T ASK HER TO TRUST HIM.
HE MADE IT FEEL FOOLISH NOT TO.

Real dominance isn't loud. It doesn't beg, boast, or barter. It moves through the room like it already belongs there. She watched him—not because he demanded it, but because he made it impossible not to.

He didn't have to win her over. He simply gave her no reason to doubt—and every reason to follow.

47.

SHE WORE ELEGANCE LIKE
ARMOUR—UNTIL HE TOUCHED HER
WITH SOMETHING GENTLER THAN
SHE'D EVER KNOWN.

Some women protect themselves with grace. Composure becomes camouflage. But real strength isn't what resists touch—it's what recognises when it's safe to yield.

He didn't disarm her or break her defences. He gave her a reason to lower them, to feel unarmed without fear. That's the difference.

48.

HE DIDN'T CHASE HER ATTENTION.
HE STUDIED HER ABSENCE.

The loud ones fall for the spotlight. The wise ones notice the shadows. He saw what she withheld—what she didn't say, didn't show, didn't offer. And that's where he set his focus.

Because a man who understands dominance doesn't need to be seen first. He watches. Learns. And when he moves—it matters.

49.

SOME WOMEN SUBMIT TOO EASILY.
THAT SHOULD NEVER BE YOU.

Submission means nothing if you hand it to anyone with a firm voice and a little nerve. Don't mistake dominance for depth. Don't trade discernment for attention.

Make them prove themselves. Then make them prove it wasn't luck.

50.

THE ONES WHO TALK THE MOST
ABOUT CONTROL ARE USUALLY THE
ONES WHO'VE NEVER HAD IT.

Real dominance doesn't need decoration. It doesn't puff its chest or narrate its every move. A man who is in control never has to say so.

It's the insecure ones who perform. Who posture. Who convince—because they're hoping someone else will believe it before they stop pretending.

51.

HE DOESN'T RAISE HIS VOICE.
HE DOESN'T HAVE TO.

True authority walks in silence. The kind that holds a room without lifting a finger. It's not about volume—it's about weight.

If a man needs to shout, it's because something in him knows he's not being heard.

52.

SHE DIDN'T KNEEL BECAUSE HE TOLD HER TO. SHE KNELT BECAUSE SHE TRUSTED HIM.

Obedience isn't submission. Real surrender doesn't come from commands—it comes from conviction.

When she knelt, it wasn't about him being in charge. It was about her choosing someone worthy to follow.

53.

IF YOU'RE ALWAYS EXPLAINING YOUR DOMINANCE, YOU DON'T HAVE ANY.

A man who knows his place doesn't need to announce it. He shows it—through restraint, clarity, presence.

If you keep needing to be understood, it's time to ask if you've actually earned it.

54.

NOT EVERY MAN WHO WANTS TO
LEAD DESERVES A FOLLOWER.

There's no shortage of men who crave control—but far fewer who can carry it. Leadership isn't about power. It's about proof—through consistency, discipline, and self-respect.

Before you follow anyone, watch how they handle themselves when no one's looking.

55.

A MAN WHO CAN'T CONTROL HIMSELF HAS NO BUSINESS TRYING TO CONTROL HER.

It starts with discipline. If his mood swings, his words lash, or his patience cracks under pressure—he's not leading. He's reacting.

Before a man earns authority over another, he should first prove mastery over himself.

56.

SHE TESTS HIM BECAUSE SHE NEEDS
TO KNOW HE WON'T FOLD.

Strength invites pressure. It's not defiance—it's verification. She isn't looking to break him; she's looking to believe in him.

If a man crumbles when challenged, he was never strong enough to carry her trust in the first place.

57.

CALLING YOURSELF A DOMINANT
DOESN'T MAKE YOU ONE. BEING ONE
DOES.

Titles are cheap. Integrity isn't. A Dominant doesn't posture or perform—he acts with purpose, speaks with weight, and leaves no question about where he stands.

It's not a label you wear. It's a standard you embody.

58.

SHE DOESN'T WANT A PERFECT MAN.
SHE WANTS A STEADY ONE.

Perfection is a lie. What she's watching for is consistency—his tone, his word, his presence. She needs to know that he won't waver when things get difficult.

She doesn't need him to shine. She needs him to stay.

59.

SHE DIDN'T GIVE HERSELF AWAY.
SHE OFFERED HERSELF SLOWLY,
LIKE A GIFT UNWRAPPED BY STEADY
HANDS.

True submission isn't theatrical. It's quiet. Deliberate. A decision made piece by piece, when safety outweighs fear and presence silences doubt.

She wasn't conquered. She was received.

60.

A DOMINANT WHO NEEDS TO BE
OBEYED IS ALREADY INSECURE. A
REAL ONE IS OBEYED WITHOUT
NEEDING TO ASK.

Commanding presence isn't about barking orders—it's about who you are when you walk into the room. A man who's worth following doesn't need constant reminders of his role.

Respect flows to those who hold themselves with quiet certainty. Not desperation.

61.

SHE TESTED HIM—BUT ONLY ONCE.
WHAT FOLLOWED WAS TRUST, OR IT
WAS NOTHING.

A true submissive doesn't linger in challenge. She asks her question with silence, stillness, or subtle resistance—and watches how he responds.

If she's still poking the edges after his answer, she wasn't submissive to begin with.

62.

THERE'S NO SUCH THING AS A BRAT.
ONLY DISRESPECT DRESSED UP AS
KINK.

Defiance isn't charming. It's a warning sign. True submission refines a woman—it doesn't give her license to misbehave under the guise of play.

And any man who indulges that chaos isn't in control. He's complicit.

63.

SOME MEN THINK SUBMISSION IS GIVEN TO WHOEVER ASKS FOR IT. THAT'S WHY THEY NEVER GET IT.

There's nothing automatic about devotion. You don't get to speak the part and skip the weight of it. A submissive gives herself to standards, not scripts.

When you carry the role like a crown and not a costume, she'll see the difference.

64.

SHE DIDN'T WANT TO OBEY. SHE
CHOSE TO. THERE'S A WORLD
BETWEEN THE TWO.

There's no power in forced obedience. Real submission only has meaning when it's freely given—when she could have walked away, but didn't.

That's where the depth lives. Not in control, but in mutual certainty.

65.

A MAN WHO NEEDS HER SUBMISSION
TO FEEL LIKE A MAN ISN'T ONE YET.

If you rely on her obedience to validate you, you've missed the point. Dominance doesn't complete a man—it reveals the man who was already there.

She's not your crutch. She's your mirror.

66.

NOT EVERY 'SIR' IS EARNED. NOT EVERY KNEEL IS SINCERE

This world is full of masks and mimicry. Surface gestures mean nothing without substance behind them. Just because she calls him sir doesn't mean she respects him.

And just because she kneels doesn't mean she's surrendered.

67.

SHE ISN'T A CHALLENGE TO
CONQUER. SHE'S A DEPTH TO BE
EARNED.

Some men confuse resistance with defiance. They chase her submission like a prize to win instead of a bond to deserve.

But the real ones understand—she's not there to be broken. She's there to be trusted with.

68.

REAL DOMINANCE HAS NOTHING
TO PROVE AND EVERYTHING TO
UPHOLD.

The man who keeps score is already losing. Dominance isn't about constant affirmation—it's about quiet consistency. It's not proven through control but through composure.

He doesn't need to win. He needs to be unwavering.

69.

SHE DOESN'T ACT OUT.
SHE LEANS IN.

A woman in true submission doesn't need chaos to be seen. Her power is quieter, her signals subtler. She leans into his stillness, not his attention.

Obedience, for her, isn't performance. It's peace.

70.

HE DIDN'T RAISE HIS VOICE.
HE RAISED THE STANDARD.

Dominance doesn't shout. It doesn't beg to be respected. It simply exists—anchored, immovable—and invites others to rise or fall by it.

A man in control doesn't need to speak loudly. His presence does the work.

71.

IF YOU HAVE TO CHASE HER
OBEDIENCE, YOU NEVER HAD HER
SUBMISSION.

Obedience isn't a reward to be begged for—it's a reflection of trust, earned over time.

If she withholds it like leverage, it was never real to begin with.

And no true Dominant would ever tolerate that game.

72.

A TRUE SUBMISSIVE DOESN'T
MAKE HIM PROVE HIMSELF
OVER AND OVER.
SHE REMEMBERS THE ANSWER
THE FIRST TIME.

Testing once is natural. Repeating the test is manipulation.

A submissive who truly trusts does not question him at every

turn—she trusts his pattern, not just his promise.

Doubt that lingers isn't submission. It's unrest.

73.

HE DOESN'T PUNISH TO FEEL
POWERFUL. HE PUNISHES BECAUSE
PEACE REQUIRES ORDER.

Correction isn't cruelty. It's protection. A Dominant doesn't act out of ego—but out of a responsibility to maintain structure, direction, and calm.

His hand is never careless. His intent is never emotional.

74.

SOME WOMEN WANT THE TITLE.
OTHERS LIVE THE TRUTH.

Anyone can call themselves submissive. It's the easiest role to pretend and the hardest to uphold. The real ones don't flaunt the label—they honour the posture, even when no one is watching.

And he sees the difference.

75.

PUNISHMENT ISN'T ABOUT ANGER.
IT'S ABOUT ALIGNMENT.

The purpose of correction isn't to vent frustration—it's to restore order. If discipline is driven by emotion, it stops being structure and starts becoming abuse.

A true Dominant corrects for the good of the dynamic. Not the satisfaction of his pride.

76.

NOT EVERYTHING IS PLAY. SOME OF
IT IS REAL.

There's a line between performance and principle. It's one thing to explore fantasies. It's another to build something rooted in discipline, trust, and unshakable clarity.

The deepest submission isn't staged—it's lived.

77.

YES, EVERY DYNAMIC IS DIFFERENT.
NO, NOT EVERYTHING IS VALID.

There's a growing lie that all expressions of BDSM are acceptable as long as they're consensual. But consent without structure is chaos—and chaos without purpose is dangerous.

There are rules. And they matter.

78.

HE DIDN'T RAISE A HAND UNTIL
HE SAW SHE WAS WORTHY OF THE
WEIGHT.

Impact play, discipline, physical control—they're not casual.

They require calibration, consent, and clarity of who she is.

No man of honour strikes without meaning.

And no true submissive seeks pain without purpose.

79.

NOT EVERYONE WHO WANTS TO BELONG, SHOULD.

This path isn't for everyone. It's not therapy. It's not rebellion. It's not some aesthetic lifestyle to collect like a hobby. The weight of dominance, the surrender of submission—these are earned positions.

Wannabes dilute what the real ones die to protect.

80.

BEFORE YOU BIND HER WRISTS,
UNDERSTAND WHAT IT MEANS TO
HOLD HER MIND.

The physical restraints are easy. They're props. What matters is the mental hold—earned through consistency, integrity, and restraint.

He leads her thoughts, not just her body. And that takes far more than rope.

81.

IF YOU'RE NOT PREPARED TO CARRY
THE WEIGHT OF HER SURRENDER,
DON'T INVITE IT.

True submission is sacred. She's handing you access to parts of her no one sees—vulnerabilities she doesn't name aloud. That kind of trust is not a toy.

Dominants who aren't ready for responsibility should never pretend they are.

82.

A FLOGGER IN HIS HAND DOESN'T
MAKE HIM A DOMINANT. IT JUST
MAKES HIM ARMED.

Anyone can pick up a tool. Not everyone has the authority to use it. It's not the implement—it's the man behind it. His self-control. His clarity. His purpose.

Impact without meaning is just violence. And there's no honour in that.

83.

SHE WANTS TO FEEL THE EDGE—BUT
ONLY WHEN SHE TRUSTS THE HAND
THAT HOLDS IT.

A submissive may crave intensity, but not recklessness. What excites her isn't the act itself—it's knowing the man behind it is sure, measured, and capable.

The more she trusts him, the deeper she can fall.

84.

THIS ISN'T PERFORMANCE.
IT'S A CALLING.
IT'S TRUTH AND POWER—
EARNED AND LIVED.

The titles, the rituals, the play—it can all look theatrical to outsiders. But for those who belong, this life is built on something ancient and disciplined.

If you're just dressing up, step aside. This isn't for you.

85.

HE DOESN'T LEAD HER THROUGH
FEAR. HE LEADS HER THROUGH
CERTAINTY.

Fear is the weapon of the weak. Certainty is the tool of a true Dominant. She follows him not because she's scared, but because she knows—his direction is sure, his control is earned.

Power built on fear always collapses. Certainty endures.

86.

NOT EVERYONE WHO LIKES
CONTROL IS A DOMINANT.
SOME ARE JUST INSECURE.

There's a difference between taking control and needing control. One is grounded. The other is panicked, performative, constantly proving something.

Dominance isn't about control for its own sake. It's about stability.

87.

PLAY HAS RULES. WITHOUT THEM, IT ISN'T SAFE.

AND IT SURE AS HELL ISN'T REAL.

The idea that anything goes under the guise of 'kink' is dangerous. Real Dominants use structure, negotiation, and aftercare. Real submissives understand limits—and why they matter.

If there are no boundaries, it's not play. It's recklessness.

88.

OBEDIENCE ISN'T ABOUT SAYING YES. IT'S ABOUT SAYING YES WHEN IT MATTERS.

Surface-level compliance means nothing if she folds at convenience but resists when it's real. True obedience shows when the moment's hard, the instruction's uncomfortable, and the trust has to mean something.

That's when submission is proven.

89.

HE DOESN'T NEED TO DOMINATE
EVERY WOMAN. HE ONLY NEEDS ONE
WORTH THE WEIGHT.

The mark of an insecure man is how many he tries to control. The mark of a true Dominant is discernment. He knows most aren't fit to kneel—and he's not interested in training the unwilling.

He isn't chasing numbers. He's building a bond.

90.

THE ONES WHO LAUGH AT RULES
ARE ALWAYS THE FIRST TO BREAK
UNDER PRESSURE.

Discipline exists for a reason. Rules aren't restrictions—they're structure. The ones who mock them don't last, because they were never built for anything real.

Real D/s dynamics aren't about chaos. They're about command. Without it, everything falls apart.

91.

A SUBMISSIVE DOESN'T NEED TO BE BROKEN.

SHE NEEDS TO BE UNDERSTOOD.

The idea that submission begins with breaking is flawed. She's not a wild creature to crush—she's a woman with depth, restraint, and fire. If you don't understand her, you'll misuse her.

A good Dominant sees through her—not over her.

92.

IF HE CAN'T MASTER HIMSELF, HE
HAS NO RIGHT TO MASTER HER.

Every Dominant begins with discipline over himself. His moods, his lust, his power. Without it, he's just a man pretending to be something he really isn't.

Leadership isn't dominance. Control isn't command. You either lead by example—or you don't lead at all.

93.

PAIN SHOULD NEVER BE A SHORTCUT
TO CONNECTION.

Some men use pain to compensate for what they lack—depth, presence, patience. But pain is a language, not a substitute. And she'll know the difference.

The right woman only gives herself to a man who doesn't need pain to reach her.

94.

THE DYNAMIC STARTS LONG BEFORE THE COLLAR.

Titles mean nothing if they aren't backed by truth. A collar isn't the beginning—it's a confirmation. The real work is in the discipline, consistency, and connection that came before.

She doesn't kneel for fantasy. She kneels for certainty.

95.

A TRUE SUBMISSIVE DOESN'T ACT
OUT. SHE OPENS UP.

Brat behaviour isn't real submission—it's insecurity in costume. A real submissive tests early, then surrenders fully once trust is earned. She doesn't play games to get attention.

She offers obedience like a gift—because she means it.

96.

A SAFE WORD EXISTS BECAUSE HE
KNOWS HIS STRENGTH.

It's not a sign of weakness. It's proof of structure. The more powerful he is, the more carefully that power must be contained—and agreed upon.

Safe words aren't just about protection. They're about mutual respect.

97.

NO ONE SELF-CROWNS IN
THIS WORLD.
YOU EITHER LIVE IT—OR YOU'RE
NOTHING.

You don't become a Dominant just by saying you are.

Calling yourself a cute name doesn't make you a submissive.

This world sees through you.

Those who live this life see through the act.

And in this world, pretenders don't last.

Either your actions carry weight—

or your title is just noise.

98.

HE TRAINS HER BODY, YES—BUT MORE THAN THAT, HE TRAINS HER FOCUS.

Obedience doesn't live in muscles. It lives in the mind.

Posture, position, protocol—all of it teaches her attention, direction, presence.

He's not here to control her. He's here to shape her.

99.

SHE DOESN'T NEED PUNISHMENT
EVERY TIME SHE FALTERS. SHE NEEDS
TO BE HELD ACCOUNTABLE.

Correction isn't always about impact.

Sometimes, it's about words. Silence. Structure. Reflection.

A true submissive wants to be held to a standard—and a real Dominant never lets her fall below it.

Accountability is how she grows.

100.

HE LEADS WITH COMMAND, NOT CRUELTY. SHE FOLLOWS WITH PRIDE, NOT FEAR.
AND TOGETHER, THEY BUILD SOMETHING NO OUTSIDER COULD EVER UNDERSTAND.

This life isn't for show. It's not for approval. It's not even for explanation. It's for those who know—those who've built it from the inside, with discipline, truth, and trust.

Let the rest watch. They wouldn't survive it anyway.

CONCLUSION

This book was not written to convince.

It was written to confirm.

For those who live this life with integrity—and for those

just beginning to learn with honour—

the path continues.

Walk it with weight. Lead with presence.

Earn everything.

And never forget:

She already knows the difference between a Dominant,

and a man who's simply trying to play one.

ABOUT THE AUTHOR

Rajan Dominari has been part of the BDSM lifestyle for over two decades. He is a respected educator, speaker, and consultant whose work is rooted in lived experience—not borrowed theory.

In 2012, Rajan launched the blog Dominant Desires, offering sharp insight into power dynamics, masculine leadership, and the unspoken structure of D/s relationships. Since then, his work has reached tens of thousands—through essays, and private mentorship.

He writes not for tourists, but for those with skin in the game. For those living this life, or learning it with honour.

Originally from London, England, Rajan now lives in Chicago, IL. He can often be found drinking a strong gin and tonic, thinking in silence, or imagining the sound of a flogger landing just right.

To learn more, visit: DomDesiresOfficial.com

CONTINUE THE JOURNEY

If *For Those Who Know* stirred something in you—
Welcome to the Darkside: A BDSM Primer
will help you ground it.

This foundational book explores the mindset, rituals,
and core principles behind healthy, powerful
Dominant/submissive relationships.

Whether you're starting from curiosity or conviction,
Welcome to the Darkside offers structured guidance
with clarity and no apologies.

Available from Raven Row Press